OSCAR
The Singing Cow

Written by
Meagen Couture

Illustrated by
Kathrin Ess

Self-Publisher
Meagen Couture

Author
Meagen Couture

Illustrator
Kathrin Ess

Designer
John Koziatek

Printer
IngramSpark

ISBN
978-0-57837-924-1 (Hardcover)

LCCN
2022910567

First Edition 2022

For Oscar, who reminded
me that being different,
is something to be cherished.

Oscar was different than any other cow.
His left horn was broken, and when he
walked, he leaned a little to one side.

Oscar also liked to sing. Loud songs, slow songs, silly songs—even opera!

The other cows ate grass from the fields all day.
Oscar loved to eat the leaves from the trees in the
forest as he sang a snazzy, jazzy tune.

The other cows were brown and black. Oscar looked
at his shaggy fur, singing, "Oh how can I, cow can I,
be all wh-wh-whiiiiiiite?"

The other cows laid in the sun by the farm.
Oscar liked to play by the lake in the woods,
while he practiced his perfectly imperfect
pitch, "Moo-la-la-LA!"

He would listen to the birds chirping and
chime in with his long, low, "MoOooOoos."
But there was no one to chime in with him.

Oscar wished he had a friend to sing and play with. Solo singing was starting to feel lonely. He needed a partner for a duet! Oscar galloped to a group of cows in the meadow. "Will you sing with me?" he asked. "Sorry, we're busy eating," one replied and lowered her head to eat more grass.

Oscar trotted to a big, black bull.
"Will you sing with me?" he asked.
"Sorry, I am busy protecting my herd,"
the bull replied. Oscar walked alone
for what felt like forever. He finally
saw another group of cows. "Would
you all like to sing with me?" he asked
doubtfully. "Sorry, we must care for
our babies," replied the mother cow.

Oscar slowly walked his crooked walk back into the forest.

When he reached the lake, he hung his head low and a single tear dropped from his eye. The birds watched sadly, and whistled a slow, hopeful tune. Oscar sung along, "MooOOooOoo... Oh, I'm so bluuuuueeeee..."

MooOoOoo...

All of a sudden, an unfamiliar voice joined in perfect harmony. "MooOoOoo, I'll sing with youuuuuuu!"

Oscar turned red. "You sing toOooOO?" he sang bashfully. "Oh yeah yeah, I dooOOoooOO!" Mable sang proudly.

She popped out of the bushes and swung the bell from her neck, "Dong-do-dong-donggggg."

She flashed a big smile. Oscar looked at her.

Mable looked different from any of the other cows he had seen. She was tiny. She didn't have any horns yet! She was not brown, or black, or white. She was grey.

"Will you be my friend?" she asked, out of breath.

Oscar paused.

"Why of course! Yes!"

Oscar danced.

Mable jumped and kicked.

Oscar and Mable walked into the forest together. They splashed in the lake.

They ate leaves from the trees.
They sang with the birds.

They lived and they laughed,
perfectly imperfect.

At the end of the day, they stared at the stars together.

"Thanks for being my friend," Mable said to Oscar.

"Thanks for being mine too," smiled Oscar.

About the Author

Meagen Couture is a hardworking mother of three. She has an education in forensic psychology and in early childhood development. As an upcoming children's book author, she strives to educate children around the world with different social emotional skills. Meagen loves music, animals, and children, and spends her free time traveling, following her heart wherever it may take her.

About the Illustrator

Kathrin Ess is a writer, painter and illustrator who lives and works in Berlin, Germany. Many years ago she traveled to Scotland, where she fell in love with the hairy highland cows. She couldn't resist when asked if she would draw Oscar. Kathrin is also the author and illustrator of her own children's book, *The Playground Under the Sea*.

www.ingramcontent.com/pod-product-compliance
Lightning Source LLC
Chambersburg PA
CBHW040712150426

42811CB00061B/1854